D1716797

THE REAL
Genghis Khan

Virginia Loh-Hagan

45th Parallel Press

Published in the United States of America by Cherry Lake Publishing
Ann Arbor, Michigan
www.cherrylakepublishing.com

Reading Adviser: Marla Conn MS, Ed., Literacy specialist, Read-Ability, Inc.
Book Designer: Felicia Macheske

Photo Credits: © ahmetnkececi/Shutterstock.com, cover, 1; © camilkuo/Shutterstock.com, 5, 30; © sirnength88/Shutterstock.com, 7; © hasachai/Shutterstock.com, 9; © Yavuz Sariyildiz/Shutterstock.com, 11; © Arctic Phoenix/Shutterstock.com, 12; © Chanwit Whanset/Shutterstock.com, 15; © Jun Mu/Shutterstock.com, 17; © Marzolino/Shutterstock.com, 19; © Porta Nicolas/Shutterstock.com, 20; © withGod/Shutterstock.com, 23; © Tom Wang/Shutterstock.com, 24; © ahmetnkececi/Shutterstock.com, 27; © gionnixxx/iStock.com, 29

Graphic Elements Throughout: © iulias/Shutterstock.com; © Thinglass/Shutterstock.com; © kzww/Shutterstock.com; © A_Lesik/Shutterstock.com; © MegaShabanov/Shutterstock.com; © Groundback Atelier/Shutterstock.com; © saki80/Shutterstock.com

45th Parallel Press is an imprint of Cherry Lake Publishing.

Library of Congress Cataloging-in-Publication Data

Names: Loh-Hagan, Virginia, author.
Title: Genghis Khan / by Virginia Loh-Hagan.
Description: Ann Arbor, MI : Cherry Lake Publishing, [2018] | Series: History
uncut | Includes bibliographical references and index. | Audience: Grades 7-8.
Identifiers: LCCN 2018004552| ISBN 9781534129504 (hardcover) | ISBN
9781534131200 (pdf) | ISBN 9781534132702 (pbk.) | ISBN 9781534134409
(hosted ebook)
Subjects: LCSH: Genghis Khan, 1162-1227—Juvenile literature. |
Mongols—Kings and rulers—Biography—Juvenile literature.
Classification: LCC DS22 .L625 2018 | DDC 950/.21092 [B] —dc23
LC record available at https://lccn.loc.gov/2018004552

Cherry Lake Publishing would like to acknowledge the work of The Partnership for 21st Century Skills.
Please visit www.p21.org for more information.

Printed in the United States of America
Corporate Graphics

Table of Contents

CHAPTER 1

Genghis Khan
The Story You Know

Genghis Khan was from Mongolia. Mongolia is between Russia and China. Khan was a great warrior. He was a great leader. He led the Mongol Empire. An empire is a group of nations ruled by a single leader. The Mongol Empire was one of the world's largest empires. Khan fought in many wars. He united the tribes in northern China. He conquered more land than anybody in history. He killed many people. He made a path through Asia and Europe. He connected east and west. He had great ideas. He paved the way for modern thinking. Modern means new and fresh. But there's more to his story...

Genghis Khan was known as the founding father of Mongolia.

CHAPTER 2

The Making of a Man

Genghis Khan was born in 1162. He was born fighting. He held a blood clot in his fist. Mongolians thought this meant he'd be a great leader.

Khan was born along the Onon River. He was named Temüjin. This means "of iron." In 1206, he was named Genghis Khan. This means "supreme leader."

Khan had a rough childhood. His father was chief. He was poisoned by Tatars. Tatars were an enemy tribe. Khan was only 9. He and his family were left to die. They were poor. Khan learned to hunt. He learned to gather. He learned to survive. Some stories say he killed his half-brother. They fought over food.

Little is known of his early life. There weren't many written records.

SETTING THE WORLD STAGE

1162

> Thomas Becket was from England. In 1162, King Henry II made him the archbishop of Canterbury. This was England's top church position. Becket fought with King Henry II. He supported the church over the king. This made the king mad. Becket was killed in 1170.

> Frederick I was the king of Germany. He was the king of Italy. He was the Holy Roman emperor. He was also called Frederick Barbarossa. Barbarossa means "red beard." In 1162, he captured Milan, Italy. He destroyed the city. He scattered its people among 4 cities.

> Ibn Zuhr was an Arab Muslim doctor. He died in 1162. He did tests on animals before working on humans. He was the first to make this a science. He first recorded mites. This led to the study of microbiology. He described throat and stomach cancers. His work developed the medical field.

Tribes fought each other. There were many wars. There were many raids. Khan grew up in violence.

Mongolians married to make peace. They did this to form **alliances**. Alliances are like teams. Khan married Börte. Börte was from another tribe. She was kidnapped. He rescued her. Around age 20, he was captured. He became a slave. Then, he escaped. People heard about him. They heard he was a good warrior. They thought he was a hero. They joined him. Khan created an army. He made peace with many chiefs. He brought tribes together.

Mongolians were nomads. Nomads are people who move around a lot.

CHAPTER 3

Military Man

Khan's army had more than 80,000 fighters. They were well-trained. They used weapons. They shot arrows while riding horses. They were fast. They were fierce. They killed about 40 million people. They destroyed cities. They kidnapped women.

Khan was a smart fighter. He studied his enemies. He took ideas from them. He won enemies over. Then he put them in charge. He looked at war like a science. He studied ways to get better.

He used **tactics**. Tactics are strategies. He shocked enemies. He pretended to quit. Then, he'd attack. He planned surprise attacks. He took hostages. He used humans as shields. He asked people to **surrender** or die. Surrender means to give up.

Khan's army rode horses. They signaled each other with large drums and flags.

Khan believed knowledge was power. His spy network helped him win wars. He called this the **yam**. The yam was well-organized. It was a system of **huts**. Huts were like stations. Huts were placed all over the empire.

Riders went from hut to hut. They carried messages. They acted as scouts. They spied on enemies. They kept tabs on what was happening. They covered about 200 miles (322 kilometers) a day. They changed horses at each hut.

This system brought supplies to everyone. It gave Khan information. It protected people as they traveled. It opened trade. It led to today's **postal** system. Postal means mail.

Huts were the first post offices.

All in the Family

Hoelun was Khan's mother. She was kidnapped during war. Yesugei was Khan's father. He claimed Hoelun. He made her his chief wife. The chief wife gave birth to the heirs. She had 5 children. She had 4 sons and one daughter. Her husband died. No one wanted to help her. She didn't give up. She took leadership of her family. She gathered food. She taught her children to fish and hunt. Her family grew strong. Hoelun advised Khan. She took care of children who lost parents in Khan's wars. She adopted them. She made them part of her family. She helped to rule while men were at war.

"If you're afraid, don't do it. If you're doing it, don't be afraid!"
— Genghis Khan

CHAPTER 4

A Born Leader

Khan was more than a killer. He also knew how to rule. He had new ways of thinking. He was born into a **feudal** world. Feudal means there are classes. Rich people ruled. Poor people worked for the rich. Khan believed in **merit**. Merit means skills. Khan rewarded loyalty. He rewarded good work. He promoted people based on skills. He didn't care about class.

He was a rich man. But he gave away his riches. He gave it to his fighters. This made the empire strong. People spent money. They bought things. This meant people had jobs.

Khan was good at finding smart and talented people.

THAT
Happened?!?

A derby is a horse race. The Mongol Derby started in 2009. It's the toughest horse race. It's the world's longest horse race. It's more than 620 miles (998 km). It goes through Mongolia. It follows Genghis Khan's postal system. The path is tough. It includes mountain passes. It includes valleys. It includes wooded hills. It includes crossing rivers. It includes dunes. It includes grasslands. The exact path is a secret until race day. Riders spend about 14 hours a day on their horses. They ride for 10 days. They camp out at night. They get 30 Mongolian horses. They get a support team. They get training. They must change horses every 25 miles (40 km). They change at support stations. They deal with harsh weather. They're tired. Many riders get hurt. They fall off their horses. They break bones. Not many finish the race.

"Although you inherited the Chinese Empire on horseback, you cannot rule it from that position." – Genghis Khan

He created **yassa**. Yassa is a code of law. He banned stealing. He banned cheating. He banned lying.

He educated his people. He created a writing system. He made everyone learn it. He made everyone use it.

He supported free trade. He thought trade joined people together. He turned cities into trade centers. He created a trade system between east and west. This was called the Silk Road. It was the main trading path. He let Europeans come to China. Khan gave them Asian **goods**. Goods are things. This trade made the Mongolians rich. Khan charged taxes. He charged **tolls**. Tolls are fees for passing.

Khan helped nature. He banned bathing in rivers. He banned littering.

CHAPTER 5

Man of Peace

Khan was known as a man of war. He was brutal. He was violent. But he could also be a man of peace.

He banned **torture**. Torture is the hurting of living things. Khan didn't hurt prisoners. There are stories about him. Some people say Khan used human skulls to build buildings. They say he boiled people alive. Historians think these are lies. The lies helped Khan win wars. People were scared. They surrendered more easily.

Khan banned slavery. He didn't let his people enslave other Mongolians. He banned the stealing of Mongolian women. He banned the selling of Mongolian women.

Torturing prisoners was a common thing to do at this time.

He believed in freedom of religion. He let people believe whatever they wanted. He gave tax breaks to churches.

This made sense. Mongolians believed many different religions. Making them believe the same religion would be impossible.

This was a tactic. Khan knew this would make people happy. People like peace more than war. They'd be less likely to **rebel**. Rebel means to fight back. Khan knew he had to accept how people lived.

But Khan had a rule. His word was the word of God. His people had to obey him absolutely.

Khan worshipped spirits in the sky, winds, and mountains.

Bad Blood

Ala ad-Din Muhammad II conquered many lands. He was the ruler of the Khwarezmid Empire. He ruled lands around the Middle East. He made a deal with Genghis Khan. Khan wanted to trade. They made a treaty. A treaty is an agreement. Khan sent men to trade. Muhammad didn't trust them. He thought they were spies. He captured the men. Khan asked him to free his men. Muhammad said no. He killed them. He broke his treaty with Khan. Khan got mad. He felt betrayed. He wanted revenge. He invaded. He led an army of 150,000 men. He destroyed cities. He killed millions of people. He took over the lands. He destroyed Muhammad II's empire. This happened in 1219 to 1221. Muhammad is known for inciting this Mongol invasion.

"A man's greatest joy is crushing his enemies."
— Genghis Khan

CHAPTER 6

Family Man

Khan's first wife was Börte. She was the **empress**. Empress is the female ruler of an empire. Khan and Börte had 4 sons. They had 5 daughters. Their family grew. They expanded the Mongolian empire. They ruled over the empire.

Khan had a large **harem**. Harem is a group of women. Khan took over lands. He took the most beautiful women from each tribe. Some say he had more than 3,000 women in his harem. He had 500 wives. He married daughters of leaders. He had many children.

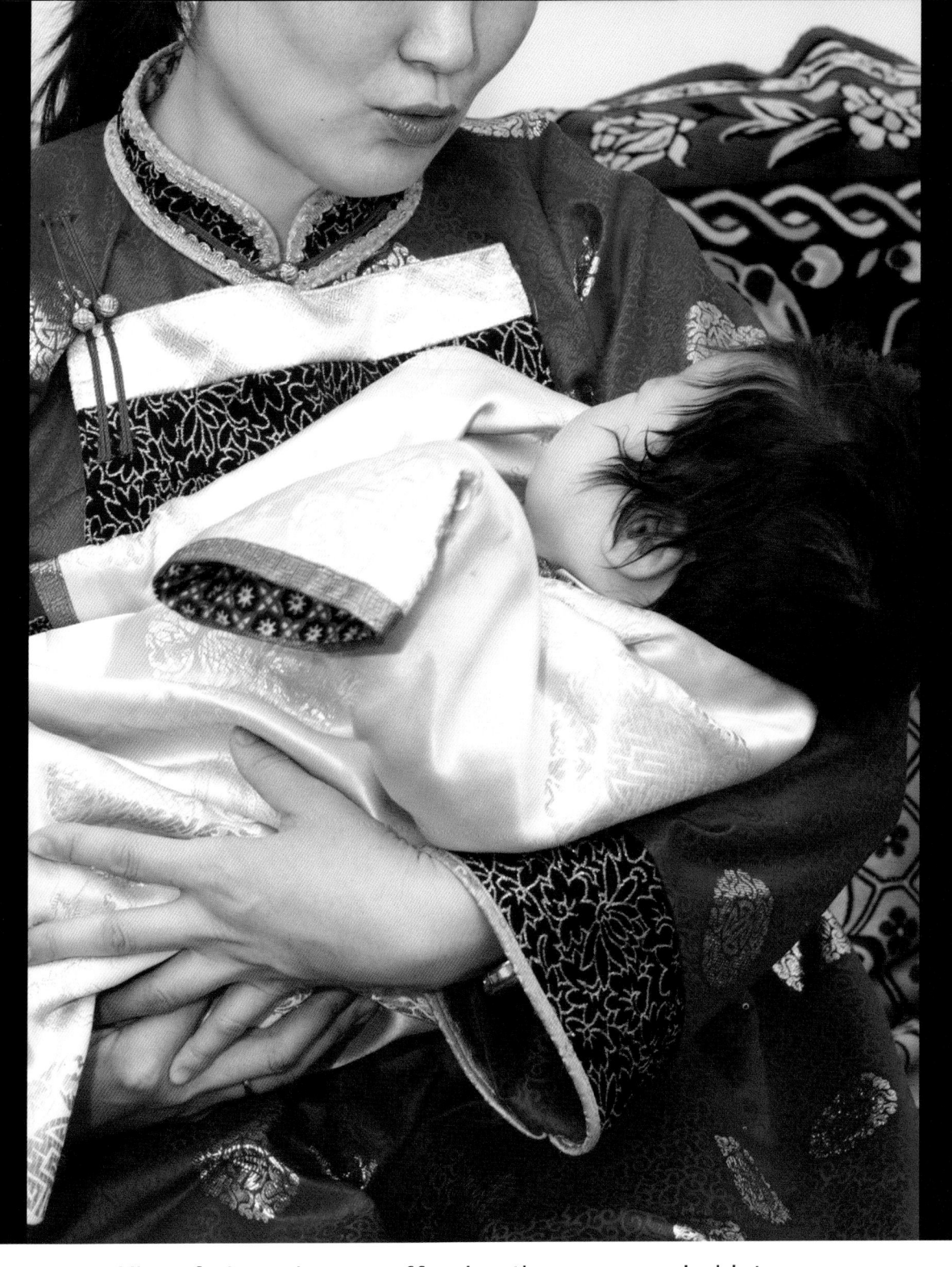

Khan fathered more offspring than anyone in history.

Khan believed a man's strength is his children. His children had children. The males had many wives. They had many children. His oldest son had 40 sons. His grandson had more than 20 sons. Khan's family kept growing. More marriages meant more children.

Descendants are people who are born from the same family line. Scientists say Khan has 16 million male descendants. They say 1 in 200 men living today are related to Khan. These men live in central Asia. Most Mongolian rulers are related to Khan.

◀ Those related to Khan call themselves "golden descendants."

CHAPTER 7

Secret Death

Khan died in 1227. His death is a **mystery**. A mystery is something unknown. No one knows how Khan died. But there are stories.

Most people think Khan fell off a horse. He was fighting in a war. His horse threw him to the ground. Khan got hurt. His organs were crushed. He never healed. He died.

Some people think he died in a hunt or war. An arrow shot him. It hit him in the knee. Khan got sick. He died.

Some people think a Chinese princess killed him. Khan tried to kidnap her. The princess had a small knife. She stabbed him. Khan died.

In 1227, Khan was too old to fight in a war.

Explained by
SCIENCE

Trees grow. New growth makes a layer of cells. Each layer is a ring. Each ring marks a year. Scientists study tree rings. They figure out the years rings were formed. They study the weather at that time. They study weather changes. Some scientists studied Mongolian tree rings. They learned why Genghis Khan was successful. During his rise to power, the weather was good. It was good for 15 years. This meant there was more food. There was more grass. There were more horses. Khan and his people were well fed. They used the horses. They could travel easily. This helped Khan win wars. Before this time, there were droughts. Droughts are dry, hot weather. No food grew. People were hungry. They were angry. Amy Hessl is a scientist. She said, "The transition from extreme drought to extreme moisture strongly suggests that climate played a role in human events."

"There is no value in anything until it is finished."
— Genghis Khan

No one knows where Khan is buried. Khan wanted this to be a secret. A small group buried his body. They took him to his gravesite. They killed anyone they saw on the way. That way, no one could spread news. The group buried Khan's body. They rode horses over his grave. This hid the place.

People have been trying to find the grave. Some think the grave is by a mountain. Some think treasures are buried with him.

Mongolians don't want his grave to be found. Some think the world will end if it is found. They want to respect Khan. They think Khan is Mongolia's greatest hero.

Being buried without markings is a tradition of Khan's tribe.

Timeline

1162 Khan was born. He was named Temüjin. He was named after the Tatar chief. This chief was captured by his father.

1178 Khan married Börte. His father had arranged the marriage. He did this before he was poisoned.

1184 Khan's wife was kidnapped. Khan called his brothers. They worked together. They rescued her. This inspired Khan to be a conqueror.

1185 Khan's first son was born. His name was Jochi. Some believe Khan wasn't his father. They think Jochi's father is the man who kidnapped Börte.

1209 Khan fought his first war outside of Mongolia. He attacked the kingdom of Xi Xia in northwestern China. Khan won. This was the start of the Mongolian invasion of China.

1211 Khan fought against the Jin family. The Jin ruled northern China. This war lasted more than 23 years.

1226 Khan's oldest son died. Jochi betrayed Khan. Some think Khan had him killed.

1226 Khan fights in his last war. He fought against northwestern Chinese tribes.

1227 Khan died. Some people think his body was taken to his birthplace.

Consider This!

Some people think Genghis Khan was a bad man. He killed a lot of people. He destroyed towns. But some people think he was a good man. He unified people. He led people. He inspired people. Learn more about him. Make a list of how he was good. Make a list of how he was bad. Do you think he was a good or bad man? Argue your point with reasons and evidence.

Most of what we know about Genghis Khan comes from *The Secret History of the Mongols*. It's the oldest known work of Mongolian history. It was written soon after Khan's death. Learn more about it. Explain why it's important.

Mongolians celebrate Genghis Khan's birthday. They celebrate on the first day of the first winter month. They made it a national holiday. Learn more about this day. What happens? Whose birthday would you like to make a national holiday? Explain why.

Learn More

Demi. *Genghis Khan*. New York: Marshall Cavendish, 2009.

Goldberg, Enid A., and Norman Itzkowitz. *Genghis Khan: 13th-Century Mongolian Tyrant*. New York: Franklin Watts, 2008.

Medina, Nico, and Andrew Thomson (illust.). *Who Was Genghis Khan?* New York: Grosset & Dunlap, 2014.

Glossary

alliances (uh-LYE-uhns-ez) teams with a common goal; pacts

descendants (dih-SEN-duhnts) offspring; sons and daughters; future generations

empire (EM-pire) group of nations ruled by a single leader

empress (EM-pris) female ruler of an empire

feudal (FYOOD-uhl) a system in which a class of aristocrats rule and the poorer classes work to serve them

goods (GUDZ) products; things to be traded

harem (HAIR-um) a group of women associated with the same man

huts (HUHTS) houses or stations

merit (MER-it) having skills or value deserving of praising

modern (MAH-durn) new; fresh; up-to-date

mystery (MIS-tur-ee) something unknown

postal (POH-stuhl) relating to a mailing system

rebel (REB-uhl) to fight against

surrender (suh-REN-dur) to give up

tactics (TAK-tiks) strategies

tolls (TOHLZ) fees for traveling or passing through

torture (TOR-chur) to hurt or harm on purpose

yam (YAM) a well-organized spy network with stations to share messages quickly

yassa (YAH-suh) code of law

Index

About the Author

Dr. Virginia Loh-Hagan is an author, university professor, former classroom teacher, and curriculum designer. She's a Chinese-American. She likes learning about Asian people and history. She lives in San Diego with her very tall husband and very naughty dogs. To learn more about her, visit: www.virginialoh.com.